MOROCCO TI
GUIDE 2023

The ultimate guide to disco ⌐ring Morocco's hidden treasures with tips for a safe trip

Steven C. Prince

Table of Contents

Chapter 1

Introduction to Morocco

A short story from my friend Emma

Emma had a never-ending appetite for adventure and had always been enthralled by the world's secrets. She had been to many locations because of her restlessness, but shc had never been to the fascinating country of Morocco. Emma set off on a voyage that would drastically change her life, determined to see the vivid colors, rich culture, and stunning scenery she had read so much about.

Emma was instantly welcomed by a tapestry of smells, sounds, and images that assaulted her senses as soon as she landed in Morocco. Spices and the lovely perfume of jasmine flooded the air, tempting the senses. The sounds of street musicians, bartering merchants, and children playing in the winding alleyways brought the busy medinas to life.

Marrakech, a place famed for its thriving marketplaces and gorgeous architecture, was Emma's first destination. She was enthralled by the bustling ambiance of the famed Djemaa el-Fna plaza. While telling stories of love, valor, and old legends, snake charmers entranced their reptilian friends. As Emma wandered the maze-like lanes of the medina, decked with vivid fabrics, sparkling lanterns, and beautiful mosaics, she became enmeshed in a frenzy of strange sights and sounds.

Emma walked into the tranquil splendor of the Atlas Mountains after leaving the metropolis behind. The sky was kissed by towering peaks, whose ragged shapes showed the passage of time. She traveled down scenic valley trails past terraced fields of vivid green that clung to the slope and tumbling waterfalls that whispered their secrets. The people welcomed Emma into their houses with warm smiles and genuine hospitality, allowing her to sample their traditional mint tea and listen to tales of their ancestors.

Emma traveled from the highlands to the captivating Sahara Desert. The sun was setting as she rode a camel, coloring the sky a brilliant orange and a delicate pink. The continuously extending sands changed shape and sculpted themselves into ethereal forms. Emma set up camp in the middle of the desert, where the brilliant stars shone down over the huge sands. She was in awe of the quiet, which was only interrupted by the wind's soft whispers, and she felt extraordinarily connected to the cosmos.

Emma found comfort in the rhythmic pounding of waves on the shore at Essaouira, a coastal town renowned for its serene beaches. She took a leisurely walk around the defensive walls as she saw fishermen mending their nets and birds circling in the clear sky. Emma's heart was calmed by the vivid blue boats floating in the port, which stood out sharply against the whitewashed buildings.

Emma pondered the beauty she had seen as her stay in Morocco came to an end. She understood that Morocco was more than simply a location; it was a combination of spectacular natural beauty, energetic cultures, and the friendliness of its people. She had been deeply moved in ways she had never anticipated.

Emma said goodbye to Morocco with a sad heart and memories seared in her memory, knowing that it will always retain a particular place in her heart. The sights, smells, and sounds of a place that had grabbed her mind as she boarded the aircraft inspired her to seek out further experiences and learn about the beauty that lay concealed in every part of the world.

1.1 Location and Geography

North Africa is home to the nation of Morocco. To the west and north, respectively, it is flanked by the Atlantic Ocean and the Mediterranean Sea. Here are some of Morocco's main geographic characteristics and locations:

1. Atlas Mountains: Spanning Morocco from southwest to northeast, the Atlas Mountains divide the nation into the Sahara Desert, the lush plains and plateaus, and the Atlantic coast.

2. Sahara Desert: The Sahara Desert, one of the world's biggest deserts, covers the southeast region of Morocco. It is renowned for its enormous sand dune fields and dry environments.

3. Coastal Regions: Morocco has a substantial coastline that stretches into both the Atlantic and Mediterranean Seas. Rugged cliffs, gorgeous beaches, and port towns like Casablanca, Rabat, and Agadir define the Atlantic coast. Cities like Tangier and Al Hoceima may be found along the Mediterranean coast.

4. Cities: Rabat, the capital, is situated on the Atlantic coast and is one of Morocco's main cities. Other significant towns include Casablanca, which serves as the nation's commercial center, Marrakech, which is renowned for its lively marketplaces and historical landmarks, Fes, which is well-known for its ancient medina (old town), and Tangier, which serves as a gateway to Europe and is home to a variety of cultures.

5. Strait of Gibraltar: The Strait of Gibraltar links the Atlantic Ocean to the Mediterranean Sea and is situated between Spain and Morocco. The strategic significance of this little canal, which has powerful currents, is well recognized.

6. Rivers: Morocco has a number of rivers, with the Draa, Moulouya, and Sebou rivers being the most notable. These rivers provide the nation with water for agriculture and sustain a number of different habitats.

7. High Atlas: With peaks rising beyond 4,000 meters (13,000 feet), the High Atlas is the tallest mountain range in Morocco. With its snow-capped peaks, deep canyons, and verdant valleys, it has a beautiful landscape.

8. Oases: Oases may be found in Morocco's arid areas. These are lush, supported by subsurface water supplies, places with flora and date palm plantations.

Geographically speaking, Morocco is diversified, including coastal regions, mountains, deserts, and fertile plains. The country's outstanding natural beauty and cultural legacy are influenced by this variety.

1.2 A Short History

Morocco has a lengthy and complicated past that has been influenced by several civilizations, empires, and cultures. An outline of Moroccan history is provided below:

1. Prehistoric History: The area that is now Morocco has been inhabited for a very long period. Later, Phoenicians, Carthaginians, and Romans settled there. The modern-day country of Morocco was part of the Roman province of Mauretania Tingitana.

2. Arab Conquest: Arab forces marched over North Africa in the seventh century, bringing Islam to the continent. Following the Umayyad Caliphate, Morocco joined the Abbasid Caliphate.

3. Dynasties and Kingdoms: Throughout Morocco's history, from the eighth to the sixteenth century, a number of dynasties and kingdoms rose and fell, including the Idrisid dynasty, the Almoravids, the Almohads, and the Marinids. These kings founded Islamic nations and left a lasting impact in terms of architecture and culture.

4. European Influence: In the 15th century, European nations like Portugal and Spain started to build commercial outposts along the coast of Morocco. Cities like Ceuta, Tangier, and Mazagan (now El Jadida) were all under Portuguese rule. However, Moroccan resistance ultimately resulted in the Portuguese being driven out and the Saadi dynasty being founded in the 16th century.

5. French and Spanish Protectorates: Morocco was a target of European imperialism in the late 19th century. Morocco was split into protectorates of France and Spain in 1912. Spain ruled the north of the nation, but the French owned a bigger chunk of it.

Morocco won independence from France and Spain in 1956, ushering in the modern era. Sultan Mohammed V ascended to the throne, and a constitutional monarchy was established in the nation. King Hassan II, who succeeded him as king and oversaw political and economic changes for over four decades.

7. Recent Developments: King Mohammed VI rose to the throne in the early 2000s and enacted further reforms, including advancements in infrastructure, education, and human rights. Additionally, Morocco has taken a lead in local issues and participates in African Union and Arab affairs.

Moroccan culture has been shaped throughout the course of its history by the Berber, Arab, and Amazigh (native North African) peoples. The language, gastronomy, music, and customs of the nation all reflect this cultural variety. Morocco is currently a well-liked travel destination because of its fascinating history, thriving towns, and breathtaking scenery.

1.3 Traditions and Culture

Moroccan culture is dynamic and diversified and is inspired by a fusion of Arab, Berber, and

Amazigh customs. Some significant facets of Moroccan culture and traditions are as follows:

1. Islam: Islam is the most common religion in Morocco, and it significantly influences the culture and traditions of the nation. Mosques play an important role in Moroccan society, since Sunni Muslims make up the majority of the population. The whole nation observes Islamic principles and customs, including as Ramadan (the month of fasting).

2. Hospitality: The generosity and cordial hospitality of Moroccans toward visitors are well-known traits. Visitors are often welcomed with tea and cookies when they enter a Moroccan house. Moroccan hospitality is based on the sharing of food and lively conversation.

3. Cuisine: Moroccan food is tasty and varied, and it draws on Mediterranean, Berber, and Arab gastronomy. Couscous, tagines (slow-cooked stews), pastilla (a savory pie), and different grilled meats are examples of signature foods.

Aromatic spices like cumin, coriander, and saffron are popular in Moroccan cuisine.

4. Moroccan Traditional attire: The djellaba is the country's most recognizable piece of traditional attire, however regional variations exist. Both men and women may be seen wearing the djellaba, a loose, hooded garment. In addition, women may choose to dress up for important occasions by donning kaftans, which are beautifully embroidered garments.

5. Music and Dance: The variety of Moroccan music represents the country's blending of cultures. Traditional music encompasses styles like Gnawa music, Berber music, and classical music from Andalusia. Popular Moroccan dancing styles include the beautiful belly dance as well as the vivacious and rhythmic Gnawa dance.

6. Morocco has a strong legacy of arts and crafts. Moroccan artists are renowned for their dexterous metal, pottery, leather, and woodwork.

The beautiful tilework and geometric motifs of traditional Moroccan buildings are also well-known.

7. Holidays and Festivals: Morocco observes a number of religious and cultural holidays. Eid al-Fitr, which commemorates the conclusion of Ramadan, is one of the most significant Islamic celebrations. Other holidays include the Birthday of Prophet Muhammad (Mawlid al-Nabi), the Islamic New Year (Eid al-Adha), and the Feast of Sacrifice (Eid al-Adha). Additionally, residents and foreign tourists are drawn to cultural activities and music festivals like the Gnaoua World Music Festival in Essaouira.

8. Souks and marketplaces: Moroccan culture is inextricably linked to traditional marketplaces known as souks. Spices, fabrics, handicrafts, and traditional Moroccan wares are among the many items sold in these thriving markets. In the souks, haggling is a regular habit, so tourists are urged to do thus in order to get better deals.

Morocco's rich history and the mixing of many influences throughout the ages are reflected in its culture and traditions. The traditions and cultural variety of the nation add to its distinct allure.

1.4 Communication and Language

Arabic, especially the Darija dialect of Moroccan Arabic, is the official language of Morocco. Other languages are used and spoken throughout the nation, nevertheless. What you need know about language and communication in Morocco is as follows:

1. Arabic: Formal contexts, government organizations, the media, and educational institutions all utilize standard Arabic. The most extensively spoken and understood language among the populace is Moroccan Arabic, or Darija. Darija is a dialect of Arabic that has its own lexicon, pronunciation, and syntax.

2. Amazigh Languages: Morocco has a sizable Amazigh (Berber) linguistic population. Tamazight, Tashelhit (Souss Berber), Tarifit (Rif Berber), and other Amazigh dialects are among those spoken. Along with Arabic, Amazigh languages are recognized as official, and initiatives have been taken to encourage their use and preservation.

3. French: The official language of Morocco and one that is extensively utilized in government, business, and education. Due to the nation's colonial background, it has historical value and is still a vital language for communication, especially in metropolitan areas and among educated people.

4. English: English is also spoken, particularly in tourist hotspots, big cities, and by those engaged in cross-border business. Many Moroccans, especially those who work in the tourist sector, speak some English.

5. Multilingualism: It's typical for Moroccans to speak more than one language, and many of them are proficient in two or more. Communication between various linguistic groups within the nation is made possible by the country's linguistic variety.

6. Non-Verbal Communication: In Morocco, like in many other cultures, non-verbal communication is important. In order to transmit meaning, demonstrate respect, and express emotions, people utilize hand gestures, facial expressions, and body language.

7. Cultural etiquette: In Moroccan culture, formality in communication and civility are valued. It is customary to shake hands while introducing yourself, and it is polite to use titles or honorifics, particularly when speaking to senior citizens.

8. Moroccan Sign Language: The country's deaf population uses Moroccan Sign Language (MSL). MSL is a vital form of communication

for the deaf community and has its own vocabulary and syntax.

In general, Morocco's language and communication reflect the country's multiculturalism and historical influences. The main languages are Arabic and Darija, although there are also considerable uses of French, English, and Amazigh in diverse situations of everyday life.

Chapter 2

Preparing for Your Trip to Morocco

2.1 Visa requirements

I can provide you an overview of Moroccan visa requirements as of the knowledge cutoff date of September 2021. The appropriate Moroccan embassy or consulate should always be contacted to confirm the most recent information since visa regulations may have changed since then.

1. Visa Exemptions: For a limited time, citizens of a select group of nations are not need to get a visa in order to visit Morocco. It is crucial to verify the particular rules for your country since

this exemption differs based on nationality. In general, visitors from nations without visa requirements are permitted to remain in Morocco for up to 90 days for leisure or business.

2. Visa on Arrival: At the Moroccan airport or border crossing, several nations that aren't visa-exempt may receive a visa. With this choice, you may get a visa that is normally valid for a shorter time than standard visas after you are in the nation. It's important to ascertain if your nation qualifies for a visa on arrival since this option may not be accessible to all nationalities.

3. Pre-Approved Visa: Prior to flying to Morocco, nationals of those nations who are not qualified for visa exemption or visa on arrival must submit an application for a visa. You may apply for a visa at the Moroccan embassy or consulate in your country of residence. A completed application form, passport pictures, a current passport, documentation of lodging in

Morocco, a trip itinerary, financial statements, and a visa cost may all be needed. Depending on the purpose of your trip, there may be different criteria and visa categories (such as a tourist, business, or student visa).

It's crucial to keep in mind that visa requirements might change and that extra restrictions can apply based on your nationality, your intended use for visiting Morocco, and the length of your stay. For the most recent and accurate information on visa requirements for your particular situation, contact the Moroccan embassy or consulate closest to you or visit their website.

2.2 When to Go There

Depending on your tastes and the activities you want to do while there, there is no one perfect time to visit Morocco. Morocco's diversified terrain, which includes coastal regions, the Atlas Mountains, and the Sahara Desert, contributes to the country's varying climate. When choosing the ideal time to travel, keep the following things in mind:

1. Spring (March to May) is typically regarded as the best season to go to Morocco. With blossoming landscapes and agreeable temperatures, the weather is moderate and pleasant. It's a great time to visit places like Marrakech, Fes, and Casablanca and go on excursions to the Atlas Mountains and the desert.

2. Summer (June to August): Morocco's summers may be quite hot, particularly in the interior and in the desert. However, coastal towns like Tangier and Essaouira benefit from a cooling sea wind. If you want to spend time by the seaside or at higher elevations in the Atlas Mountains, summer might still be a nice season to come if you can stand the heat.

3. Fall (September to November): The fall is another favored season for Moroccan travel. As

the day cools down, the weather is still excellent for visiting numerous places. Outdoor pursuits like mountain climbing or camel riding in the desert are ideal at this time of year.

4. Winter (December to February): Although Morocco's winters are generally moderate, temperatures may drop precipitously at night, particularly in the country's hilly and desert areas. It's still fun to go during this season to coastal regions and towns like Marrakech and Fes, but if you want to go to the desert, be ready for chilly evenings.

Morocco is a year-round vacation destination, and each season has its own special appeal. However, bear in mind that during the busiest travel times, major tourist locations might get congested. Additionally, you should organize your trip appropriately if you have interests in certain occasions or festivals, such as the Kelaat M'Gouna Rose Festival or the Marrakech International Film Festival.

The ideal time for your trip to Morocco will depend on the weather, activities, and crowd levels that you enjoy.

2.3 Tips for Health and Safety

The importance of putting your health and safety first while visiting Morocco cannot be overstated. Observe the following health and safety advice:

1. see a Travel Health expert: To acquire the most recent information on Morocco-specific health precautions and required vaccinations, it is advised that you visit a travel clinic or see a travel health expert before your trip.

2. Drink plenty of water: Morocco's weather may become hot, especially in the summer. Drink enough of bottled water to stay hydrated and refrain from using tap water or beverages with unidentified ice.

3. Safe Food and Drink Consumption: Watch what you eat and drink. Avoid eating raw or undercooked food, street food from unsanitary stalls, and unpeeled fruits and vegetables unless they have been well cleaned. Instead, stick to well-cooked meals. Drink bottled water, and stay away from ice-filled drinks from shady vendors.

4. Sun protection: Wear a hat, sunglasses, sunscreen with a high SPF, and light, breathable clothes to shield oneself from the intense Moroccan sun. During the warmest times of the day, seek shade and remain hydrated.

5. Travel Insurance: Having travel insurance that pays for medical costs, vacation cancellations, and lost or stolen possessions is strongly advised. Make that your insurance policy is up to date, covers your requirements, and is valid for Morocco.

6. Transportation Security: Use cautious if you decide to use public transportation or hire a driver. Select authorized taxis and make sure

they utilize the meter or have a fee in mind before the trip. For longer journeys, use trustworthy transportation services, or think about hiring a trustworthy tour guide.

7. Cultural Sensitivity: Honor Moroccan traditions and culture. When visiting religious locations, especially, dress modestly and be aware of regional traditions and customs. Before shooting pictures of anybody, particularly ladies, get their consent.

8. Preventing small Theft: Just as in other tourist area, remain aware of your possessions and take safety measures to avoid small theft. Be careful in crowded spaces, lock your valuables, and keep pricey goods hidden.

9. Emergency Contact Information: Learn the Moroccan emergency phone numbers for the police, ambulance services, and the embassy or consulate of your nation.

10. COVID-19 Safety Measures: COVID-19 is a worldwide problem as of the cutoff date in September 2021, to my understanding. Maintain up-to-date knowledge of the COVID-19 situation in Morocco, abide by regional regulations, and practice proper hygiene by using masks, keeping a safe distance, and often washing your hands.

Prior to your journey to Morocco, don't forget to check for any recently updated travel advisories or health warnings from your government or relevant authorities. You can travel safely and enjoy yourself in Morocco by being prepared and exercising prudence.

2.4 Currency and Financial Issues

Here are some crucial things to have in mind about money and currencies in Morocco:

1. Money: The Moroccan Dirham (MAD) is the country of Morocco's official currency. Upon

arriving in Morocco, it is recommended to convert your money into Moroccan dirhams. Since the dirham is a closed currency, it isn't often used or exchanged outside of Morocco. Banks, exchange bureaus (bureaux de change), and approved hotels all provide currency exchange services.

2. Exchange Rates: Because exchange rates vary often, it's wise to research the most recent rates before your travel. Currency exchange services are often available at large airports, banks, and exchange bureaus. In order to be sure you're receiving a fair bargain, it is advised to compare rates and fees.

3. Cards and Cash: Although most hotels, bigger restaurants, and stores in popular tourist destinations take credit and debit cards, it's always a good idea to carry some cash, particularly in smaller towns or local markets where cash is more often used. Cities and towns are replete with ATMs where you may use your

debit or credit card to withdraw money in Moroccan dirhams.

4. Inform Your Bank: Before leaving for Morocco, let your bank or credit card provider know that you'll be there. By doing this, they can't mark your purchases as suspicious and may ban your card for security purposes.

5. Small Denominations: Because it may be difficult to receive change for bigger notes in certain locations, it's a good idea to keep smaller denominations of Moroccan Dirhams on hand for minor purchases, taxi costs, and gratuities.

6. Safety Advice: Use care while using ATMs or transporting cash. Keep an eye out for danger, protect your PIN while using an ATM, and keep your money and credit cards safe. For increased security, it is recommended to utilize ATMs that are housed within banks or other recognized businesses.

7. Limitations on Foreign money Exchange: Generally, there are no limitations on the quantity of foreign money you may carry into Morocco. However, while entering or leaving the country, you must disclose any sums that exceed MAD 100,000 or the equivalent.

8. Tipping is customary in Morocco, especially for hospitality services like restaurants, hotels, and tours. Although not required, it's usual to offer a tip of 10% or more for excellent service. Make sure you have enough Moroccan dirhams in smaller quantities on hand for tipping.

Keep an eye on your spending and set a budget that works for you. When handling money, use caution at all times and keep an eye out for scams or fake bills. For detailed guidance on currency conversion and overseas transactions, it is essential to speak with your local bank or financial institution.

Chapter 3

Getting to Morocco

3.1 International Flights

Morocco is a well-liked destination for international flights as of my knowledge cutoff in September 2021, and it has multiple international airports that act as entrance points for tourists. Morocco's principal international airports are as follows:

1. Mohammed V International Airport (CMN) is the busiest airport in Morocco and a significant hub for international travel. It is close to Casablanca.

2. The Marrakech Menara Airport (RAK) is another significant international entry point for

travelers to Morocco and is located in Marrakech.

3. Agadir-Al Massira Airport (AGA): This airport, which is in Agadir, is a key entryway for travelers traveling to southern Morocco.

4. Tangier Ibn Battuta Airport (TNG): This airport, which is close to Tangier, is well linked to a number of European cities and acts as a crucial hub for visitors to the northern portion of Morocco.

5. Fes-Sass Airport (FEZ): This airport serves Fes and the surrounding areas by providing international flights to and from a number of locations. Most of its customers are tourists exploring the old city.

Many international airlines fly into these airports, linking Morocco to many locations throughout Europe, Africa, the Middle East, and beyond. Please take notice that since my last update, flight times, routes, and admission criteria may have changed. For the most recent information on international flights to Morocco, it is always essential to check with the airlines and relevant authorities.

3.2. Transportation by Land and Sea

Travelers may use Morocco's well-developed land and maritime transportation systems.

Buses are a common means of transportation in Morocco. Land Transportation: 1. The nation has a vast bus network that connects important cities, villages, and tourist locations. Both intercity and intracity bus services are offered by organizations like CTM, Supratours, and other private operators.

2. Trains: Morocco's ONCF (Office National des Chemins de Fer) operates a dependable rail network across the country. Major cities including Casablanca, Rabat, Marrakech, Fes, Tangier, and others are connected by the railroad

network. In general, Moroccan trains are pleasant and provide various levels of service.

3. Taxis: In Moroccan cities and towns, taxis are readily accessible. Petite taxis and large taxis are the two main categories. Grand taxis are bigger and may be hired for interstate travel, whilst petite taxis are smaller and often red-colored vehicles that operate only inside municipal borders.

4. Rental Cars: If you want to explore rural parts of Morocco or want the freedom to go at your own leisure, renting a vehicle is a practical alternative. In significant cities and airports, several automobile rental companies are present.

1. Ferries: Morocco's coastline is home to various ports that provide ferry services to and from Europe. The busiest ferry lines go from Tangier to Tarifa or Algeciras, connecting Morocco with Spain. These ferry services are run by organizations including FRS, Balearia, and Acciona Trasmediterranea.

2. Cruise Ships: Mediterranean or Atlantic-bound cruise ships often stop in Morocco. Cruise itineraries often include ports like Casablanca, Tangier, and Agadir, enabling travelers to see the nation on shore excursions.

It's crucial to keep in mind that there may be changes to the available transit choices and schedules, so it's always a good idea to check for the most recent information, particularly with respect to any travel limitations, routes, and schedules.

3.3 Moroccan Transportation

You may travel across Morocco utilizing a variety of transportation options. The following are some popular methods for getting across the nation:

1. Buses: Within Morocco, buses are a well-liked means of transportation for both short

and long distances. There are several bus kinds available, including local buses that service certain towns and areas and intercity buses run by organizations like CTM and Supratours. Buses link large cities, villages, and tourist locations and are often inexpensive.

2. Trains: The ONCF (Office National des Chemins de Fer) runs Morocco's well-developed rail system. For travel between major cities like Casablanca, Rabat, Marrakech, Fes, Tangier, and others, trains are a convenient and pleasant choice. First class and economy grades of service are available on the railway system.

3. Taxis: In Moroccan cities and towns, taxis are readily accessible. Petite and big taxis are the two different categories of taxis. Petite taxis are little, often red taxis that only go short distances inside cities. Grand taxis are bigger and have more seating capacity. They are often used to go to farther-flung locations or for interstate travel.

4. Rental cars: Renting a vehicle is a well-liked choice for tourists who want the freedom to drive to isolated places of Morocco and want to experience the country at their own speed. In significant cities and airports, several automobile rental companies are present. It's crucial to remember that driving in Morocco may be difficult, particularly in busy cities, and that road conditions frequently fluctuate.

5. Shared Taxis: Also referred to as "grands taxis" or "collective taxis," shared taxis are a popular means of transportation for completing shorter interstate journeys or traveling to locations that are not well serviced by buses or railways. These taxis follow predetermined itineraries and wait to leave until they have a sufficient number of clients.

6. Domestic Flights: Domestic flights are an alternative if you need to go further or swiftly reach a distant location. Moroccan airports provide domestic flights connecting the

country's main cities, enabling you to travel faster.

It's crucial to plan your routes and take into account the particular transportation alternatives available depending on your preferences and destination. Additionally, always check the most recent timetables, prices, and any applicable travel restrictions.

Chapter 4

Exploring Moroccan Cities

4.1 The Marrakech

Western Morocco's busy city of Marrakech is renowned for its lively culture, fascinating history, gorgeous architecture, and dynamic souks (markets). Listed below are some facts about Marrakech:

1. History: The Almoravid dynasty established Marrakech in the 11th century, and it was Morocco's capital for many years. The Almohads and the Saadian dynasty, among others, ruled the city at different times. The city is filled with palaces, mosques, and other historical sites that serve as reminders of its past.

2. Medina: Marrakech's medieval medina, a UNESCO World Heritage site, is the city's beating heart. The medina is a confusing network of winding lanes, crowded plazas, and historic riads (traditional Moroccan homes with an internal courtyard). The main plaza in the medina, Djemaa el-Fna, is a bustling center of activity with street entertainers, food booths, snake charmers, and market sellers.

3. Architecture: Islamic, Moorish, and Berber influences may be seen in the mix of architectural styles found in Marrakech. With its recognizable minaret, the Koutoubia Mosque is a well-known landmark in the area. The Bahia Palace, the Saadian Tombs, and the magnificent Ben Youssef Madrasa are further architectural marvels.

4. Souks: The vivid atmosphere of Moroccan markets may be experienced at Marrakech's busy souks. Spices, fabrics, pottery, leather products, and traditional Moroccan handicrafts are just a

few of the items sold at the souks. In order to get the greatest deals, be prepared to haggle in the souks.

5. Gardens: Marrakech is home to a number of lovely gardens that provide a peaceful retreat from the busy city. The Majorelle Garden is renowned for its vivid blue structures and exotic plant species. It was initially created by French painter Jacques Majorelle and subsequently became the property of Yves Saint Laurent. Other well-liked green areas worth seeing are the Menara Gardens and the Agdal Gardens.

6. food: Marrakech provides a broad variety of gastronomic pleasures, and Moroccan food is rich and eclectic. Popular traditional foods include pastilla (a salty pie), couscous, and tagines (slow-cooked stews). Don't forget to sample some Moroccan mint tea, a tasty and cooling beverage that is popular all throughout the nation.

7. Festivals & Events: Throughout the year, Marrakech holds a number of festivals and events. The Marrakech International Film Festival is one of the most well-known and draws well-known directors and celebrities from all over the globe. Another notable occasion that showcases traditional music, dance, and art is the Festival of Popular Arts.

8. Day Trips: Marrakech is a starting point for seeing other sites in the area. You may go via day excursion to the adjacent Atlas Mountains to go trekking, see Berber settlements, or just to soak in the natural beauty of the surroundings. The "Hollywood of Morocco," the desert town of Ouarzazate, is also reachable from Marrakech.

Visitors are mesmerized by Marrakech's vivid hues, exotic scents, and frenetic activity. Its distinctive fusion of hospitality, culture, and history makes it a must-see location in Morocco.

4.2. Casablanca

Morocco's capital and main commercial and financial center is Casablanca, the country's biggest metropolis. It is situated on the nation's western shore, gazing out over the Atlantic Ocean. Listed below are some details about Casablanca:

1. Modern Metropolis: Casablanca is renowned for its contemporary and international vibe. It boasts a skyline made up entirely of buildings, busy streets, and a thriving nightlife. People from varied origins are drawn to the city since it is a melting pot of numerous cultures.

2. Hassan II Mosque: The Hassan II Mosque is one of Casablanca's most recognizable structures. It is one of the biggest mosques in the world and the biggest in Morocco. Its minaret dominates the skyline of the city, rising to a height of 210 meters (689 feet). The mosque is renowned for its beautiful design, elaborate embellishments, and waterfront position.

3. Corniche: The Corniche is an oceanfront seaside walkway that runs the length of Casablanca. It is a well-liked location for taking leisurely strolls, running, or just taking in the beautiful scenery. Restaurants, cafés, and beach clubs surround the Corniche, creating a lively scene for both residents and visitors.

4. Medina: Although Casablanca is a contemporary city, its medieval medina (old town) is nevertheless interesting to explore. The medina provides a window into the city's history, despite not being as big or well-preserved as those in other Moroccan towns. You may explore its winding alleyways, go to local markets, and take in the authentic Moroccan architecture.

5. Casablanca is renowned for its distinctive fusion of architectural styles. The early 20th century French colonial period produced a sizable number of Art Deco structures in the city. Beautiful examples of this architectural type

may be seen throughout the city, particularly in the Habous Quarter district.

6. retail: Casablanca has a vast variety of retail options, making it a shoppers' paradise. Modern retail centers including Morocco Mall, Anfa Place, and Twin Center are located in the city and provide upscale items from throughout the world. Additionally, traditional Moroccan arts, crafts, fabrics, spices, and souvenirs are available in the Habous Quarter and the Central Market (Marché Central).

7. Food and Cuisine: The gastronomic scene in Casablanca is broad and includes both local fare and cuisine from across the world. The city's proximity to the seaside contributes to the popularity of seafood. Restaurants near the Corniche provide fresh fish and seafood for you to enjoy. Never pass up the opportunity to sample regional favorites like tagines, couscous, and Moroccan sweets.

8. Mohammed V plaza: Mohammed V Square is Casablanca's main plaza and is named after the country's previous monarch. It is an important meeting spot and a center of activity. The Wilaya (Governorate) and the courtroom are only two of the significant structures that surround the plaza. It's a terrific place to observe people and take in the lively vibe of the city.

With its modernism, cultural richness, and energetic environment, Casablanca provides a distinctive experience in Morocco. Casablanca has something for everyone, whether you're interested in seeing historical monuments, taking in the seaside vistas, or indulging in shopping and cuisine.

4.3 Morocco's Fes

Fes, sometimes spelled Fez, is one of Morocco's most historically and culturally important cities. Fes, a city in the northeastern region of the nation, is recognized for its exquisite Islamic history, traditional handicrafts, and well-preserved medieval old town. Here are some facts about Fes:

One of the biggest and oldest still-existing medieval cities in the world is the medina of Fes, which is a UNESCO World Heritage site. Fes el-Bali (Old Fes) and Fes el-Jdid (New Fes) are its two major divisions. The center of the medina, Fes el-Bali, is renowned for its winding alleyways, little lanes, and ancient structures.

2. The Al-Qarawiyyin Mosque and University: The Al-Qarawiyyin Mosque was built in the ninth century and houses one of the world's oldest institutions. It is a key center of culture and religion and contributed significantly to the growth of Islamic knowledge. Although non-Muslims are not allowed inside the mosque, they are welcome to see its spectacular outside construction.

3. Madrasas and Mosques: Fes is home to a large number of mosques and madrasas, which are

Islamic schools that include beautiful Moroccan architecture and elaborate tilework. The Bou Inania Madrasa, the Attarine Madrasa, and the Chrabliyine Mosque are a few famous examples. These locations provide a look into the rich architectural history and spiritual traditions of Fes.

Fes is renowned for its ancient leather tanneries, where leather is prepared using centuries-old methods. The biggest and most well-known tannery in the city is The Chouara Tannery. From terraces surrounding the tannery, visitors can watch the tanning process while also having the option to buy leather items.

5. Souks & Handiwork: Fes is recognized for its strong artisan community and traditional handiwork. You may discover a broad variety of traditional Moroccan handicrafts in the medina, which is a treasure trove of winding passageways and busy souks, including carpets, pottery, metalwork, leather products, and textiles. Discovering the souks offers the chance

to shop for one-of-a-kind handcrafted goods and see artists at work.

6. Fes events: Fes has a number of vivacious events that highlight its cultural diversity. The Fes Festival of globe Sacred Music, which takes place every year and features performances by musicians and artists from all over the globe, is the most prominent. The event unites many cultures while honoring spiritual music.

Palaces and Gardens: Fes is home to some exquisite palaces and gardens. Although the inside of the Royal Palace (Dar el-Makhzen) is not accessible to the general public, it is a striking architectural monument. The Jnan Sbil Gardens, also known as Bou Jeloud Gardens, provide a tranquil respite from the busy streets of the city and are a favorite hangout for both residents and tourists.

8. Fes food: Fes is well known for its own culinary customs. Rich and tasty Fassi tagines, exquisite pastilla (a sweet and savory pie), and

the well-known Fes medfouna (a filled bread) are just a few of the city's well-known culinary offerings. Be sure to sample the regional food and discover all of Fes's unique tastes.

With its bustling souks, interesting historical sites, and local handicrafts, Fes is a city that completely immerses tourists in the medieval allure of its old town. For those looking for a real Moroccan experience, it is a must-visit location since it provides a fascinating look into Morocco's cultural and architectural legacy.

Chapter 5

Discovering Morocco's Natural Beauty

5.1 About the Atlas Mountains

In Morocco, North Africa, there is a notable mountain range called the Atlas Mountains. It passes through Morocco, Algeria, and Tunisia for 2,500 kilometers (1,600 miles). The range serves as a natural partition between the Sahara Desert and the Atlantic coast.

The Atlas Mountains in Morocco include the following salient characteristics and details:

1. Subdivisions: There are three primary ranges that make up Morocco's Atlas Mountains: the High Atlas, Middle Atlas, and Anti-Atlas.

- High Atlas: Within the Atlas Mountains, this is the tallest and largest range. It contains Mount Toubkal, the highest mountain in North Africa, which rises to a height of 4,167 meters (13,671 ft).

- Middle Atlas: The Middle Atlas range, which lies to the north of the High Atlas, is lower in height than the High Atlas. It's well-known for its cedar trees and a well-liked spot for outdoor pursuits including hiking and animal viewing.

- Anti-Atlas: The Anti-Atlas range, which lies southwest of the High Atlas, is distinguished by untamed terrain and vast valleys. It has a lot of mining activity and abundant mineral resources.

2. Climate: Depending on height and location, the climate in the Atlas Mountains varies. In general, the higher locations have cooler temperatures and more precipitation, which includes snowfall throughout the winter. A warmer Mediterranean climate with hot, dry

summers and mild winters may be found in the lower valleys and southern slopes.

3. Biodiversity: A wide variety of plant and animal species may be found in the Atlas Mountains. The Barbary macaque, an endangered species of monkey, the Atlas cedar tree, and the Atlas mountain viper may all be found in the High Atlas. While the Anti-Atlas has distinctive desert-adapted flora and fauna, the Middle Atlas is famous for its oak and cedar woods.

4. Cultural Importance: Different Berber groups have lived in the Atlas Mountains for many years. The Berber people have created a rich cultural history and adapted to the rocky environment. Traditional Berber settlements, sometimes referred to as ksour or kasbahs, are hidden tucked away in the highlands and exhibit distinctive design and workmanship.

5. Tourism and Outdoor Activities: Adventurers and outdoor lovers often go to the Atlas

Mountains. The area provides options for mountain riding, hiking, trekking, and skiing (during the winter). Domestic and foreign visitors are drawn to the scenic scenery, quaint communities, and cultural experiences.

Overall, the Atlas Mountains in Morocco are a magnificent natural feature that provide tourists breath-taking views, opportunities for cultural discovery, and leisure pursuits.

5.2. Sahara Desert

The Sahara Desert, which spans an area of around 9.2 million square kilometers (3.6 million square miles), is the world's biggest scorching desert. Along with Morocco, Algeria, Tunisia, Libya, Egypt, Mauritania, Mali, Niger, Chad, and Sudan, it also encompasses a number of other North African nations.

The Sahara Desert's salient characteristics and details are as follows:

1. Size and Location: The Sahara Desert is enormous, spanning the Mediterranean Sea in the north to the Sahel area in the south and the Atlantic Ocean in the west to the Red Sea in the east. About one-third of the African continent is occupied by it. Huge areas of sand dunes, rocky outcrops, gravel plains, and sporadic mountain ranges make up the terrain.

2. Climate: The Sahara Desert is renowned for its severe and very dry environment. It is characterized by hot days that may reach 50 degrees Celsius (122 degrees Fahrenheit) and by chilly nights with much lower temperatures. One of the driest places on Earth, the Sahara receives very little and irregular rain.

3. Sand Dunes: The Sahara is well known for its recognizable sand dunes, which are able to soar to astounding heights. These dunes are made up of many different forms, such as long ridges called "ergs" and solitary hills called "seif dunes." The Erg Chebbi in Morocco is the most

well-known Sahara dune, drawing travelers with its breathtaking sunrises and sunsets.

4. Oasis: The Sahara is home to various oasis that are dispersed across the desert, despite its severe circumstances. These water-rich areas—often underground—allow for the development of flora and the habitation of human groups. They act as valuable resources for the neighborhood and as a pleasant respite for desert-crossing visitors.

5. Nomadic Cultures: For thousands of years, several nomadic groups have lived in the Sahara Desert. Particularly the Tuareg and Berber people have evolved a rich cultural history by adapting to the desert's environment. The primary mode of transportation for these tribes has historically been camel caravans, and they have been important participants in trans-Saharan trade routes.

6. species: The Sahara Desert sustains a remarkable amount of species despite its

difficult conditions. Unique vegetation, insects, reptiles (such the desert monitor lizard), and mammals species like the fennec fox and dromedary camel are just a few of the species that have evolved to thrive in the desert climate.

7. Tourism and adventure: Due to its breathtaking vistas and plenty of adventure opportunities, the Sahara Desert draws visitors from all over the globe. Visitor favorites include camel trekking, 4x4 desert safaris, sandboarding, and stargazing under the desert stars. Additionally, there are cultural activities offered, such as going to nomadic settlements, seeing historic places, and traveling along old trade routes.

The Sahara Desert is a magnificent natural marvel that gives visitors a picture of a huge and difficult environment that has influenced the history, culture, and ecology of the nearby areas.

5.3 The Atlantic Ocean

The coastline that runs along the Atlantic Ocean's eastern shore is referred to as the Atlantic Coast. It comprises a number of nations and areas, each with unique features and traits. The Atlantic Coast is described in the following manner:

The Atlantic Coast stretches over four continents—North America, South America, Europe, and Africa—in total. It encompasses a huge area and several nations, including the United States, Canada, Brazil, Portugal, Spain, Morocco, Senegal, and countless more.

2. Coastal Landscapes: The Atlantic Coast exhibits a broad variety of landscapes, ranging from rocky shorelines to huge marshlands and from steep cliffs to sandy beaches. Depending on the area, different characteristics may apply. For instance, the North American Atlantic Coast is renowned for its charming coastal

communities, whereas some of the African coast has expansive sandy beaches.

3. Marine Life and Biodiversity: A wide range of marine species and habitats may be found along the Atlantic Coast. Numerous species, including fish, dolphins, whales, seals, sea turtles, and different bird species, call coastal regions home. Along the coast, estuaries and wetlands provide a distinctive biodiversity and are important habitats for many creatures to reproduce.

4. Economic Importance: The economics of the areas the Atlantic Coast passes through are significantly impacted. Along the shore, the fishing and aquaculture sectors are thriving, giving coastal people jobs and food supplies. Additionally, tourism is a significant economic contributor, as tourists are drawn to the coastline beauty, leisure pursuits, and cultural attractions.

5. Cultural and Historical Importance: The Atlantic Coast has a vibrant cultural and historical past. Since many coastal places have

been inhabited for many years, distinct coastal cultures and customs have emerged. The region's marine history and commercial links are attested to by old ports, lighthouses, and fortresses along the coast.

6. leisure Activities: Both residents and tourists may enjoy a variety of leisure pursuits along the Atlantic Coast. Swimming, surfing, sailing, kayaking, fishing, beachcombing, and nature viewing are all popular pastimes. To attract visitors, coastal locations often include beach resorts, seaside villages, and recreational amenities.

7. Environmental Challenges: The Atlantic Coast suffers a number of environmental issues, including as habitat deterioration, coastal erosion, and sea-level rise. To conserve the natural beauty of the shore and save its ecosystems, these concerns need sustainable management techniques and conservation initiatives.

The Atlantic Coast is, in general, a complex and dynamic ecosystem that has great ecological, economic, and cultural importance. It is a well-liked location for both nature enthusiasts and those looking for coastal experiences due to its breathtaking vistas, rich marine life, and recreational activities.

Chapter 6

Immersing in Moroccan Cuisine

6.1 Customary Moroccan Food

Moroccan cuisine is renowned for its variety of dishes, fragrant spices, and rich tastes. Here are a few well-known Moroccan dishes:

1. Tagine: The term "tagine" describes both the cooking pot and the food that is cooked in it. It is a kind of stew that is slowly cooked and often contains meat (such as lamb, chicken, or beef), vegetables, and a blend of herbs and spices. Often, tagine foods feature a sweet and salty taste combination.

2. Couscous: A mainstay of Moroccan cuisine is couscous. It is comprised of semolina grains and often topped with a tasty stew. Spices, veggies, and meat may all be used in the stew. For Friday lunch, which is a significant meal in Moroccan culture, couscous is a common dish.

3. Pastilla (Bastilla): Pastilla is a savory pie formed from layers of thin pastry dough that are filled with a combination of spiced meat (often pigeon or chicken), almonds, and eggs. It has a distinctive sweet and savory flavor since it is sprinkled with powdered sugar and cinnamon.

4. Harira: To break the fast during Ramadan, this traditional Moroccan soup is often given. It starts with a tomato, lentil, chickpea, and a variety of spice foundation. It may also include meat (often lamb or beef), and it frequently has fresh herbs as a garnish.

5. Mechoui: Mechoui is a well-liked meal for parties and special events. Whole lambs or sheep

are carefully roasted in a special oven or over an open flame. The meat is usually served with bread and conventional dipping sauces and is soft and tasty.

6. Zaalouk: Usually served as a side dish or dip, zaalouk is a delicious eggplant and tomato salad. A tasty and fragrant meal is made by roasting the eggplant and combining it with tomatoes, garlic, olive oil, and different spices.

Briouats are little, triangular pastries that come in a variety of fillings. They may be filled with cheese, vegetables, shellfish, or meat that has been seasoned. Typically, briouats are deep-fried until they are crispy and golden brown.

8. Moroccan Mint Tea: Although Moroccan mint tea isn't really a meal, it is a crucial component of Moroccan culture and cuisine. Green tea leaves, fresh mint leaves, and sugar are used to make this delicious and energizing beverage. It is often served in little glasses and represents friendliness.

These are but a few examples of typical Moroccan cuisine. Moroccan food has a vast variety of tastes and culinary pleasures to offer.

6.2 Well-liked street fare

Morocco is renowned for its thriving street food scene, which has a huge selection of mouthwatering and tasty cuisine. The following are some of the most well-known street meals in Morocco:

1. Moroccan sandwiches, or bocadillos, are delectable flatbread sandwiches loaded with grilled meats (kefta, chicken, or beef), veggies, herbs, and sauces like harissa or chermoula. They are often served hot and are a delightful choice for street food.

Brochettes are skewers of marinated and grilled meat, often lamb or chicken, that are popular in Morocco. A mixture of spices, including cumin, paprika, and herbs, are used to season the meat, giving it amazing tastes. Brochettes are often served with grilled veggies on the side and bread.

Merguez, a spicy and savory sausage from Morocco, is produced from a combination of lamb or beef with a mixture of spices including paprika, cumin, and garlic. Typically, it is grilled and offered as a sandwich or side dish.

4. Msemen, or Moroccan pancakes, are square pancakes cooked from a mixture of wheat, semolina, and butter. It is often stacked or folded before being grilled on a griddle. Msemen may be eaten simple or filled with a variety of ingredients, such as veggies, cheese, or honey.

5. Babouche, or Moroccan Snail Soup, is a distinctive street food delicacy that is available in Moroccan towns, especially in the nights. Snails are cooked in a tasty broth that has been flavored with herbs, spices, and a little heat.

Locals see it as a delicacy and love it when served hot.

6. Moroccan Fried Fish (Sardines or Fish and Chips): You may discover delectable fried fish stands throughout Morocco's coastline. Fresh fish, such as sardines or other regional species, is floured, seasoned, then deep-fried until crispy. They often come with a side of tangy dipping sauces, bread, and fries.

7. Moroccan Fresh Fruit Juices: Morocco has a wide range of fruits, and you may buy juices made from freshly squeezed fruit from street sellers. Orange juice, grapefruit juice, pomegranate juice, and fruit smoothies are all popular choices. They are a cool option for satisfying your thirst while walking around the city.

Moroccan street cuisine would not be complete without its assortment of sweet desserts (Sellou, Chebakia). Sesame seeds, almonds, flour, honey, and spices are all used to make the traditional

Moroccan energy snack known as sellou. Chebakia is a twisted, honey-syrup-soaked fried pastry that is shaped like a flower. You can sate your sweet craving with these goodies.

These are just a few examples of common Moroccan street cuisine. A great approach to discover the country's many tastes and culinary traditions is to investigate the local street food scene.

6.3. Moroccan Tea Culture

Moroccan tea culture is fundamental to hospitality and social events and is strongly rooted in Moroccan culture. Following are some essential elements of Moroccan tea culture:

1. Moroccan mint tea, sometimes referred to as "atay b'naana," is the most well-known and recognizable kind of tea in Moroccan culture. Usually, green tea leaves, fresh mint leaves, and sugar are used to make it. In order to get a frothy

texture, the tea is boiled in a teapot with hot water before being poured into tiny cups from a height. It is renowned for having a sweet and energizing flavor.

Moroccan tea preparation is regarded as an art form, and there is a certain procedure that must be followed. Boiling water is then poured over the tea leaves and fresh mint in a teapot. The tea is put into glasses and steeped for a few minutes. To combine the tastes and produce foam, the tea is then poured back into the teapot from a height. Before the tea is ready to be served, this pouring procedure is done many times.

3. Symbol of Hospitality: Moroccan tea is a representation of hospitality and is often provided to visitors as a mark of appreciation and welcome. When visitors arrive, it is usual for the hosts to make and serve tea. Tea service and pouring are done with considerable care and are seen as kind and welcoming gestures.

4. Moroccan tea is consumed in a communal context, and it is typical for people to congregate and share tea. Around a tiny table or tray, people may often sit on cushions or low stools to enjoy their tea. It is normal for guests to partake in numerous rounds of tea while conversing and socializing with one another. The host serves the tea to the visitors.

5. Tea Time: Moroccans drink tea all day long, but there are certain occasions when it is especially loved. Tea is often consumed in the late afternoon, during lunchtime, and after supper. Moroccan tea is often provided during religious and cultural events like Ramadan and weddings.

6. Moroccan tea etiquette: When consuming Moroccan tea, there are a few rules to follow. Using your right hand to take the tea and to hold the tea cup is considered courteous. It is also traditional to sip tea carefully and appreciate its nuances. As a further sign of kindness, it is typical to pour tea for others before oneself.

7. Tea Accompaniments: A range of accompaniments, including typical Moroccan pastries like cookies, almond candies, or salty nibbles, are often offered with Moroccan tea. These sweets enrich the whole tea-drinking experience and go well with the tea's tastes.

Moroccan tea culture plays a big role in everyday life there, bringing people together and fostering a friendly environment. It serves as a representation of Moroccan hospitality and provides a delicious taste of Moroccan customs.

6.4 Dining Manners and Traditions

Moroccan eating manners and traditions are distinctive and represent the country's rich cultural heritage. Following are some essential guidelines for Moroccan eating etiquette:

1. Handwashing: It's normal to wash your hands before eating. For this reason, a small pitcher of water and a bowl are often offered.

2. Seating Arrangements: Meals are often taken in a typical Moroccan setting while seated on cushions or low stools around a small table. Usually, everyone sits at a community table and shares the dishes that are put in the middle of the table.

3. Right Hand for Eating: Similar to many Middle Eastern and North African cultures, eating with your right hand is considered courteous. It is customary to only do personal hygiene duties with the left hand; it is not utilized for eating.

4. Sharing Food: Moroccan meals are often shared by everybody, with dishes set in the middle of the table. It is usual to use your right hand to grab food from the communal dishes and put it on your plate. It is considerate to take a

little amount of food while consuming it so that there is plenty for everyone.

5. Using Bread as a Utensil: Bread, especially the circular flatbread known as khobz, is a crucial component in Moroccan cooking. To scoop up food, particularly stews and tagines, it is often used as a spoon. Use a slice of bread you've torn off to pick up the meal instead of your fingers.

6. Hospitality and Generosity: These virtues are highly valued in Moroccan culture. You can be given generous servings of food as a guest or urged to eat more than once. Accepting such presents and expressing gratitude for the host's kindness are considered courteous.

7. Respecting Food: Food waste is typically disapproved of in Morocco, where cuisine is highly prized. It is courteous to taste a little quantity of everything that is offered and not leave a lot of food on your plate. However, if you have dietary limitations or allergies, you are

also welcome to respectfully refuse a specific meal.

8. Moroccan mint tea, which was previously noted, has a unique position in Moroccan tradition. As a sign of hospitality, tea is often provided at the conclusion of a meal. It is usual to take the tea and savor it since doing otherwise might be seen as rude.

9. Polite Gestures: In Morocco, it's polite to show your appreciation and thanks for the dinner. It's customary to express gratitude to the host or chef for their efforts and to provide compliments on the cuisine once the dinner is over.

10. Respectful Eating: Lastly, it's important to keep in mind how to eat with good table manners, which include not chatting while you're eating and keeping your mouth shut.

You may demonstrate your respect for Moroccan culture and ensure a satisfying meal experience for both you and your hosts by adhering to these rules of eating etiquette.

Chapter 7

Experiencing Moroccan Traditions

7.1 Moroccan Festivals and Celebrations

Morocco is renowned for having a rich and varied cultural past, which is seen in the many festivals and festivities held there all year long. The following are a few of the most well-known holidays in Morocco:

1. Eid al-Fitr: This festival, which celebrates the conclusion of Ramadan, the Islamic holy month of fasting, is one of the most significant religious occasions in Morocco. Gatherings of families

take place to celebrate with feasts, prayers, and gift-exchanging.

2. Eid al-Adha: Also referred to as the Feast of Sacrifice, this holiday honors Abraham's (Ibraham's) readiness to offer his son as a sacrifice to God. It entails the sacrifice of an animal, often a sheep, and the distribution of the meat to loved ones, close friends, and those in need.

3. Mawazine Festival: One of the biggest music events in Africa, Mawazine is held yearly in Rabat. In addition to traditional Moroccan music, it also includes music from other countries and well-known Western performers. The event draws visitors from all around the globe as well as locals.

4. Tan-Tan Moussem: The Tan-Tan Moussem is a customary cultural celebration honoring the nomadic origins of the Sahrawi tribes in southern Morocco. It include poetry readings,

camel beauty pageants, horse racing, and traditional dances.

5. Fes event of globe Sacred Music: This event, which takes place in Fes, brings together musicians and artists from all over the globe to celebrate spiritual music and advance interreligious understanding. The concerts are held across the city at a number of historic locations.

6. Imilchil Marriage celebration: This unusual celebration honors the custom of arranged weddings and is held in the High Atlas Mountains. Young people from various Berber tribes congregate to meet possible mates and take part in cultural dances, music, and festivities.

7. The rich Gnaoua musical legacy, which has origins in West Africa, is celebrated during the Gnaoua World Music Festival, which is held in the seaside town of Essaouira. It combines traditional and modern music by bringing

together Gnaoua musicians and well-known worldwide performers.

These are just a handful of the many festivals and events that Morocco celebrates all year long. Each festival offers a different window into the nation's rich cultural history and gives both residents and tourists a lively and unforgettable experience.

7.2. Hammams and conventional spas

Moroccan hammams and traditional baths are deeply ingrained in the country's culture and have a long, illustrious history. These locations provide a distinctive and soothing experience where visitors may declutter, revitalize, and mingle. Here is some information about Moroccan hammams and conventional spas:

1. Hammams: A hammam is a traditional steam bath used in Morocco that has a set bathing regimen. A steam room, several bathing rooms,

and a leisure space are usually included. Both public and private spaces include hammams.

- Public Hammams: Open to anyone, public hammams often include distinct areas for men and women. Locals often congregate there to socialize and practice personal hygiene. Public hammams provide a classic community bathing experience and are often more cheap.

- Private Hammams: In Morocco, there are a lot of opulent hotels and resorts with private hammams that provide a more private and unique experience. Additional amenities like massages, body washes, and aesthetic services are often offered in these hammams.

2. Spa Services: Moroccan spas are renowned for its natural and conventional services that make use of regional components and methods. Typical spa services include:

- Moroccan Bath, sometimes referred to as gommage, is an exfoliating procedure that uses black soap composed of eucalyptus and olive oil to clean and soften the skin. The body is first massaged with soap by the therapist before being scrubbed vigorously with a special mitt to remove dead skin cells.

- Rassoul Clay Treatment: Found in the Atlas Mountains, Rassoul is a mineral-rich clay. It is used to the skin during spa treatments to cleanse and detoxify it. The body and face are covered with clay, which is then washed off after drying. The result is revived and renewed skin.

- Argan Oil Massage: Argan oil, which comes from the Moroccan-native argan tree, is prized for its hydrating and nourishing qualities. To moisturize the skin, increase circulation, and encourage relaxation, it is often used during massages.

3. Rituals and customs: Moroccan hammams and traditional baths often adhere to certain rituals and customs that improve the experience as a whole. These may consist of:

- Heat and Steam: In a hammam, you spend some time in a steam chamber, which causes your body to perspire and opens your pores. This aids in both muscular relaxation and skin cleansing.

- Scrubbing: Using black soap and scrubbing mitts to exfoliate is a crucial component of the hammam experience. It helps the body rid itself of toxins, dead skin cells, and pollutants, leaving the skin glowing and smooth.

- Relaxation: Following the washing and exfoliation, people may unwind in a peaceful setting, either in a special relaxation room or by getting additional spa services like massages or facials.

The Moroccan culture and customs may be experienced while relaxing and pampering oneself in hammams and other traditional spas. Whether you go to a posh spa or a public hammam, these experiences provide a special fusion of rest, renewal, and cultural immersion.

7.3 Berber art and henna tattoos

Two distinctive facets of Moroccan culture that highlight the nation's many creative traditions are henna tattoos and Berber painting. Here are some details about Moroccan henna art and Berber tattoos:

1. Henna Tattoos: Henna, a plant-based pigment used to make temporary tattoos on the skin, is utilized to create elaborate designs. Mehndi or henna tattoos have been a part of Moroccan culture for years and are often used to mark important festivities and occasions including weddings, festivals, and religious rituals.

- Application: A cone or a tiny brush is used to apply henna paste on the skin in artistic designs. After the paste has dried and been scraped off, it leaves a reddish-brown stain that becomes darker over time. Depending on the henna's quality and how well it is taken care of, the design may endure for a few days to a few weeks.

Henna tattoos in Morocco often have symbolic meanings and come in a variety of designs, depending on the locale and the event. Geometric shapes, floral themes, and complex lace-like patterns are typical motifs. Henna is used as a decorative technique and is said to offer blessings, protection, and good fortune.

2. Berber Art: As a native ethnic group in Morocco, the Berbers have a rich creative tradition that is reflected in a variety of media, including textiles, ceramics, jewelry, and architectural design. Berber art is distinguished by its vivid hues, complex patterns, and use of organic materials.

- Textiles: Berber textiles are distinguished by their vibrant colors and intricate patterns. Geometric patterns, symbols, and motifs that signify Berber cultural identity and history are often seen on carpets, rugs, blankets, and clothes. Every location and tribe may have its own unique skills and styles.

- Berber pottery is a significant medium for creative expression. Handmade clay plates, pots, and pottery sometimes have elaborate patterns and designs, occasionally combining geometric and abstract elements. Techniques for manufacturing traditional pottery have been handed down through the centuries.

- Jewelry: Berber jewelry is very valuable due to its exceptional workmanship and symbolic meaning. A lot of jewelry is made of silver and often has elaborate engravings, beads, and vibrant gemstones. Depending on the tribe and location, jewelry designs might change, with each item symbolizing a cultural custom or conveying a tale.

- Architecture: Berber architecture has distinguishing characteristics, notably in the

Atlas Mountains and southern portions of Morocco. The walls, entrances, and ceilings of adobe homes, often referred to as ksour and kasbahs, sometimes include geometric patterns and ornamental themes. These architectural features showcase Berber cultural identity and skill.

In Morocco, henna tattoos and Berber art are both significant sources of creative expression. They not only highlight the nation's rich cultural history but also provide visitors the chance to interact with traditional art forms and learn more about Moroccan customs and symbols.

7.4 Moroccan Dance and Music

The colorful and varied music and dance of Morocco reflect the nation's rich cultural history and influences from numerous areas and ethnic groups. Here is a description of Moroccan dance and music styles:

1. Gnawa Music: Originating in West Africa, Gnawa is a traditional Moroccan musical style. It mixes rhythmic and spiritual aspects and is often used as a healing ritual. Traditional instruments like the guembri (a three-stringed lute), qarqaba (metal castanets), and drums are used in gnawa music. Call-and-response singing, mesmerizing rhythms, and vivacious dancing steps are its distinguishing features.

2. Andalusian Music: The ancient Islamic kingdom of Al-Andalus on the Iberian Peninsula is where the beginnings of Andalusian music may be found. It is a kind of classical music distinguished by complicated rhythms and complex melodies. The oud (lute), violin, qanun (zither), and percussion instruments are among of the instruments often employed in andalusian music. Ensembles made up of singers and musicians are called takht, and they are often used to play andalusian music.

3. Chaabi Music: Popular in Morocco, chaabi music is distinguished by its upbeat rhythms and

captivating tunes. It has roots in metropolitan areas and draws inspiration from both Western popular music and Moroccan folk music. Chaabi songs are sung during social gatherings and festive occasions and often include lyrics in Moroccan Arabic dialects. The violin, accordion, oud, and percussion instruments are employed in chaabi music.

4. Berber Music: The indigenous Amazigh population of Morocco is represented through berber music. Rhythmic percussion, flutes, and string instruments are often used, however it differs across locations and tribes. Themes of rural life, environment, and cultural identity are often reflected in Berber music. The ahidous dance is a well-known Berber traditional dance that is done by men and women in a circle.

5. Ra music: Originally from western Algeria, Ra music became well-liked in Morocco and other North African nations. It combines classical Bedouin music with contemporary styles including Western pop, rock, and reggae.

The passionate voices and vibrant rhythms of Ra music are often used to describe it. Due to their contributions to the genre, artists like Cheb Khaled and Cheb Mami have attained worldwide prominence.

6. Moroccan Dance: Moroccan traditional dance styles are an essential component of social gatherings and festivals of culture. Several well-liked dance forms are:

- Ahidous: As was already said, ahidous is a traditional Berber dance that is done in a circle and accompanied by chanting and drums. It is a collective dance that often conveys tales of rural life and communal harmony.

- Chikhat: Chikhat is a female solo dance form that has its roots in Moroccan cities. Seductive motions, expressive gestures, and rhythmic footwork are its defining features. At weddings and other festive gatherings, chikhat dancers often perform.

- Guedra: The Tuareg people of the Sahara Desert perform Guedra, a spiritual dance. It involves a female dancer doing dexterous motions while chanting and clapping rhythmically, often while wearing a flowing robe. Guedra dance is regarded as a kind of trance-inducing ritual that promotes healing.

- Raqs Sharqi: Also known as Oriental or Belly Dance, Raqs Sharqi is becoming more and more well-liked in Morocco. It is a solo dancing style distinguished by smooth hip, torso, and arm motions. Traditional Moroccan musical styles are often included into Raqs Sharqi.

Moroccan music and dance provide an enthralling window into the nation's cultural richness and customs. Moroccan music and dance are a dynamic and engaging way to experience the country's culture, whether it's the pulsating rhythms of Gnawa or the vigorous motions of traditional dances.

Chapter 8

Shopping in Morocco

8.1 Souvenirs and Handicrafts

Morocco is a well-liked location for gifts and handicrafts because of its rich cultural history and traditional craftsmanship. Here are some examples of the trinkets and crafts you may purchase in Morocco:

1. Moroccan Carpets and Rugs: Moroccan carpets and rugs are renowned for their exquisite handweaving. These complex items come in a variety of shapes and colors and are often manufactured using conventional processes.

2. Leather Goods: Morocco places a great priority on leatherwork, and you can find a variety of leather goods there, including wallets, belts, shoes, and purses. Particularly well-known for their leather tanneries is the city of Fez.

3. Ceramics & Pottery: Moroccan ceramics and pottery are wonderful works of art. Intricately patterned tiles, colored tagines (traditional Moroccan cooking pots), ornate plates, and bowls are also readily available.

4. Metalwork: Beautiful brass and copper trays, lamps, teapots, and ornamental objects are made by Moroccan artists using metal. The engravings and designs on the metals are very elaborate.

5. Moroccan woodwork is a display of fine workmanship and attention to detail. Beautifully carved furniture, doors, mirrors, and boxes may be found; these items are often decorated with conventional geometric designs.

Moroccan tea sets are a common gift since tea is a significant component of Moroccan culture. Typically, these sets come with a tray, cups, and a teapot. They often have vivid decorations and dexterous workmanship.

7. Traditional Clothing and Textiles: Popular Moroccan apparel includes babouches (slippers), djellabas (length, flowy robes), and kaftans. Moroccan textiles are extremely well-liked, and popular examples include woven blankets, pillowcases, and embroidered linens.

8. Moroccan Spices: A broad range of fragrant spices, including saffron, cumin, cinnamon, and paprika, are available at the lively Moroccan spice markets. These spices are excellent culinary keepsakes.

It is advised to visit neighborhood marketplaces (souks) and artisan cooperatives to discover genuine and high-quality souvenirs and crafts while shopping in Morocco. As it is normal practice in Moroccan marketplaces, keep in mind to haggle and negotiate costs.

8.2. Traditional Bazaars and Markets

Morocco is renowned for its thriving souks, or traditional marketplaces and bazaars. These vibrant markets, which sell everything from handicrafts and fabrics to spices and culinary items, are an essential aspect of Moroccan culture. The following Moroccan bazaars and traditional marketplaces are noteworthy:

1. Marrakech Medina: One of Morocco's most well-known and active marketplaces is located in Marrakech's medina. With its bustling ambiance, snake charmers, street entertainers, and many kiosks offering everything from spices and leather items to pottery and traditional attire, Jemaa el-Fnaa, as it is often known, delivers a sensory explosion.

2. Fes Medina: The medina of Fes, which is a UNESCO World Heritage site, is well-known for its eons-old labyrinthine lanes and conventional marketplaces. There are several souks in the medina devoted to different types of crafts, including leather, pottery, spices, and textiles. Also intriguing to see are the tanneries in Fes, where leather is treated and coloured.

3. Essaouira Medina: Essaouira, a seaside town, has a wonderful medina that is well worth seeing. A variety of fresh seafood, spices, fabrics, and handicrafts are available in the market in the medina. Compared to the busy medinas of Marrakech and Fes, it is more laid back.

4. Chefchaouen Medina: Known as the "Blue City," Chefchaouen's medina is renowned for its magnificent blue-painted structures. There are many different handicrafts available at this market, including handmade blankets, carpets, and regional artwork.

5. Casablanca Central Market: In this up-to-date market, people may purchase fresh fruit, meat, seafood, spices, and home goods. It offers a genuine view of everyday life in the biggest city in Morocco.

6. Agadir Souk El Had: One of the biggest marketplaces in the area is found in the beach city of Agadir. Spices, pottery, textiles, and other Moroccan things are among the many products it sells.

7. Rabat Medina: Rabat, the capital of Morocco, has a bustling market where you can buy regional goods including textiles and traditional handicrafts.

Be ready for a vibrant and somewhat packed experience while visiting these classic marketplaces and bazaars. Part of the appeal is discovering the little lanes and mingling with neighborhood traders. As it is usual in Moroccan marketplaces, remember to haggle and negotiate pricing.

8.3. Moroccan rugs and carpets

Moroccan carpets and rugs are recognized around the globe for their superb quality, unique patterns, and significant cultural heritage. These handmade fabrics are a representation of the tradition and skill of Moroccan weavers. More details on Moroccan rugs and carpets are provided below:

1. Traditional Weaving Methods: Moroccan carpets and rugs are often handcrafted utilizing age-old weaving methods that have been handed down through the centuries. The "Berber knot" or "double knot," in which each knot is made around two warp threads, is the most often used method. This method produces a thick, sturdy carpet.

2. Berber Carpets: One of the most well-known varieties of Moroccan carpets is the berber carpet. The Berber tribes of Morocco, who are

renowned for their nomadic way of life and distinctive cultural identity, are the ones that customarily weave them. Geometric patterns and symbols that symbolize elements of Berber culture and religion are often seen on Berber carpets.

3. Beni Ourain Carpets: These carpets, which come from the Atlas Mountains, are renowned for their simplistic patterns and plush texture. They often have a distinctive white backdrop with geometric designs in brown or black and are crafted from premium natural wool.

4. Carpets from the Azilal area of Morocco are known as Azilal carpets. They are renowned for their vivid hues, amorphous patterns, and artistic motifs. Azilal carpets often have a variety of vivid colors and include themes and symbols with cultural importance.

5. Kilim Rugs: Found in several Moroccan areas, kilim rugs are flat-woven carpets. They stand out for their beautiful weaving patterns and light

weight. Rugs made of kilim are often used as ornamental items or as prayer rugs.

Moroccan rugs and carpets are used for both practical and symbolic reasons. They are used to decorate furniture, floors, and walls, bringing warmth and beauty into rooms. Additionally, the patterns and symbols woven into the carpets often have religious and cultural importance, representing the beliefs and customs of the weavers and narrating tales.

7. Buying Moroccan Carpets: It is advised to purchase Moroccan carpets from reliable merchants, such as cooperatives or well-known carpet stores. These guarantee the authenticity and ethical trading of the carpets. Examining the carpet's quality, workmanship, and materials is crucial as well. The cost of Moroccan carpets might vary based on the size, level of pattern intricacy, and kind of wool used.

Owning a Moroccan carpet or rug displays the nation's rich tradition and workmanship while adding a touch of Moroccan culture and creativity to your house.

8.4 Argan Oil and Cosmetics

A highly valued beauty product with Moroccan roots is argan oil. It is made from the kernels of the argan tree, which is indigenous to Morocco's southwest. More details on argan oil and its beauty products are provided below:

1. Argan oil production: Argan oil is created via a time-consuming procedure. The interior nut of the argan fruit is manually extracted after the kernels have been picked, dried, and split. The priceless argan oil is then extracted from the nuts via cold pressing. The advantages and natural qualities of the oil are preserved thanks to this ancient technique.

2. Advantages for Skin and Hair: Argan oil is prized for its hydrating and nourishing qualities. It is abundant in vitamin E, antioxidants, and

vital fatty acids, all of which help moisturize and renew the skin. Argan oil has a reputation for enhancing skin suppleness, minimizing the look of fine lines and wrinkles, and fostering a bright complexion. In order to make hair softer, smoother, and easier to maintain, it is also used to feed and condition it.

3. Cosmetics and aesthetic Products: In addition to being offered as pure oil, argan oil is also a component of many cosmetic and aesthetic products. Numerous products, including face creams, serums, body lotions, shampoos, conditioners, hair treatments, and even oils for the cuticles and nails, are available that include argan oil. To increase their potency, these products often include additional organic components along with the healing qualities of argan oil.

4. Authenticity and Quality: It's crucial to make sure that the argan oil or cosmetic products made with it are genuine and of high quality. To verify you're receiving real argan oil, look for items

that are marked as "100% pure," "organic," or "cold-pressed." A further way to guarantee the oil is supplied ethically is to purchase from respected companies or suppliers that promote fair trade and sustainable business practices.

5. Fostering Women's Cooperatives: Moroccan women's lives have been significantly impacted by the production of argan oil. Many cooperatives for the production of argan oil have been founded, especially in Morocco's rural regions, where women are given jobs and empowerment via the process. By buying argan oil and goods made with argan oil from these cooperatives, you help these women support their lives and advance sustainable economic growth.

Due to the many advantages that argan oil and its beauty products provide for the skin, hair, and general health, they have become more popular all over the globe. You may benefit from the pure and nourishing qualities of this Moroccan gem by including argan oil into your beauty regimen.

Chapter 9

Outdoor Activities and Adventures

9.1 Trekking and Hiking

Morocco's magnificent scenery, varied terrain, and opportunity to fully experience the nation's rich culture make trekking and hiking there an amazing excursion. When organizing a hiking or trekking excursion in Morocco, keep the following important factors in mind:

1. Popular hiking Regions: Morocco has a number of well-known hiking areas, all of which provide distinctive experiences. The most well-known and easily accessible mountains for

hikers are those in the High Atlas, which include Mount Toubkal. Other well-liked options are the Rif Mountains, Middle Atlas, and Anti-Atlas. From craggy peaks and deep valleys to lush woods and ancient Berber communities, each area has its own distinctive landscape.

2. Best Time to Trek: Morocco's spring (April to May) and fall (September to November) seasons, when the weather is moderate and pleasant, are the best times to go trekking. Lower valleys may have sweltering summers, while higher elevations get snowy winters with difficult weather.

3. Trekking Routes: Depending on your interests and degree of fitness, you may pick from a variety of trekking routes. The Toubkal Circuit, which leads to Mount Toubkal, the highest mountain in North Africa, through isolated valleys and Berber communities, is a well-liked option. The Mgoun Massif, Sirwa Mountains, and Ameln Valley are further routes.

4. Your options for lodging: On multi-day excursions, you may choose to tent or stay in a mountain refuge. While camping lets you totally immerse yourself in nature, refuges provide basic necessities like food and lodging. You could also be able to enjoy a traditional Berber guesthouse in certain regions, which offers a unique cultural encounter.

5. Local Guides and Mules: Getting a local guide for your walk in Morocco is highly advised. They can secure your safety, are knowledgeable with the area, and can provide insightful information about local customs and culture. Mules are often employed to transport bulky goods and equipment, making your travel more pleasant.

6. Altitude and Physical Fitness: Trekking in Morocco sometimes includes ascending to high elevations, particularly if you're aiming to conquer Mount Toubkal. It's crucial to be physically healthy and well-prepared for the difficulties of altitude hiking. Altitude sickness

may be avoided with appropriate water and gradual acclimatization.

7. Cultural etiquette: Due to the rich cultural legacy of Morocco, it is crucial to respect the country's traditions and customs. Be respectful of local sensibilities and dress modestly while traveling through villages. Positive encounters may be promoted by saying "Salam" (hello) to locals and learning a few fundamental Arabic or Berber words.

8. Safety Considerations: Put your safety first by including essentials like good hiking boots, layered clothes, sun protection, a first aid kit, and plenty of water in your bag. It's a good idea to have a dependable map or GPS gadget and to let someone know about your hiking intentions.

9. Environmental Responsibility: It's important to lessen your influence on the environment as a responsible hiker. Respect the environment, properly dispose of garbage, and adhere to the "leave no trace" maxims. Additionally, it is

advised that you assist regional conservation initiatives and favorably influence the people you come across.

Moroccan trekking and hiking provide a fantastic chance to see the nation's many landscapes and take in its lively culture. You may make priceless memories on your Moroccan vacation if you make the necessary preparations, practice environmental stewardship, and have an open mind.

9.2 Riding a Camel in the Desert

An iconic activity that lets you fully appreciate Morocco's wide and captivating scenery is camel riding in the desert. What you should know before riding a camel in the desert is as follows:

1. Popular Desert Regions: In Morocco, the Sahara Desert is the most well-liked desert area for camel rides. The two primary locations where camel trekking is often conducted are the

Erg Chebbi dunes near Merzouga and the Erg Chigaga dunes near Zagora. Both provide amazing vistas of enormous sand dunes as well as the chance to see beautiful sunrises and sunsets.

2. The length of camel treks: Depending on your preferences, camel treks in the desert may last anything from a few hours to several days. Longer excursions allow for a deeper investigation of the desert and the opportunity to sleep beneath the stars, while shorter rides are appropriate for those who just want a taste of the experience.

3. Riding Camels: Dromedaries, which have a single hump, are the most common kind of camels used for riding in Morocco. These animals can withstand lengthy travels through sand-covered terrain and are well suited to desert environments. You will be seated in a saddle or a blanket that has been put on the back of a camel while you are being led by a knowledgeable guide behind the caravan.

4. Desert Camps: Overnight stays in desert camps are sometimes included in multi-day camel journeys. These camps vary from simple tents in the nomadic style to more opulent ones with plush beds and facilities. You can take in the tranquility of the surroundings, take in traditional music and dance performances, and relish delectable Moroccan food by spending the night in the desert.

5. Considerations for the weather: Because the desert may encounter tremendous heat, it's important to schedule your camel ride carefully. The colder months from October to April are the ideal time to go since the weather is more agreeable. Summertime temperatures may be quite high, making daytime riding difficult.

6. Sun Protection and Essentials: It's essential to take sun protection measures before going on a camel ride in the desert. To protect oneself from the harsh desert heat, put on a hat, sunglasses,

and sunscreen. Bring a lot of water with you as well so you can keep hydrated during the trip.

7. Desert Exploration: Desert excursions often provide the chance to explore the local surroundings in addition to camel riding. You could have the opportunity to do sandboarding, see local nomadic settlements, climb sand dunes, or even take in some traditional desert entertainment like falconry or music shows.

8. Photography Possibilities: With its huge stretches of sand, unusual lighting, and stunning dunes, the desert offers fantastic photo opportunities. Bring your camera or smartphone so you may document the desert's splendor and make priceless memories.

9. Environmental Respect: It's important to respect the delicate ecology and reduce your environmental effect while riding a camel in the desert. Don't disrupt animals or plants, dispose of garbage appropriately, and adhere to responsible tourist standards.

A magnificent experience, camel riding in the desert lets you get close to nature and take in the breathtaking splendor of Morocco's Sahara area. Whether you choose a quick ride or a multi-day trip, the grandeur and peace of the desert will make a lasting impression on your adventure.

9.3 Watersports and Surfing

Morocco's attractive coastline and top-notch waves have helped the sport of surfing and other water sports become more well-liked in recent years. What you should know about surfing and other water activities in Morocco is as follows:

1. Surfing Locations: Morocco's Atlantic coastline is home to a number of surfing locations. Taghazout, Tamraght, Agadir, Essaouira, and Sidi Ifni are a some of the well-known surfing locations. For surfers of all experience levels, from beginners to experts, these spots provide reliable waves.

2. ideal period for Surfing: The winter months, from October to April, are the ideal for surfing in Morocco because the swells brought on by Atlantic storms provide the finest waves during this period. However, surfing is a year-round activity in Morocco, with summer months offering fewer swells and better conditions for novices.

3. Surf Schools and Rentals: There are several surf schools along the coast whether you're new to surfing or want to improve your abilities. These institutions provide instruction for all skill levels with the aid of qualified teachers and necessary tools. For those who like to surf alone, you may hire a surfboard and a wetsuit.

4. Wave diversity: To accommodate various surfing inclinations, Morocco's coastline provides a diversity of wave types. For surfers of all skill levels, there are beach breakers, point breaks, and reef breaks. Longboarding is more appropriate in certain areas, while more

experienced riders may use the hollow barrels at other locations.

5. Other Watersports: Morocco's coastline offers options for kiteboarding, windsurfing, and paddleboarding in addition to surfing. Essaouira is popular among kiteboarders and windsurfers because of its excellent wind conditions.

6. Gear and Equipment: It is advised to bring your own surfboard and gear if you have them. The majority of surf schools and rental businesses, however, provide a variety of surfboards, wetsuits, and other essential gear if you don't already have it. Prior to renting, make careful to inspect the equipment's condition.

7. Safety considerations: Safety should always come first while engaging in any water activity. Before setting off, pay attention to the weather, tides, and currents. It's a good idea to surf with a friend, let someone know what you're up to, and consider your own ability level while picking waves to ride.

8. Beach Culture and Etiquette Observe fundamental manners and pay respect to the local beach culture. Take turns, be courteous to other surfers, and respect the queue. By properly disposing of waste and according to any applicable rules or laws, you can help keep the beaches clean.

9. Discover the Coastal villages: In addition to your surfing experience, spend some time discovering the coastal villages and getting to know the people there. savor mouthwatering Moroccan cuisine, explore lively souks (markets), and mingle with welcoming people.

Morocco's varied coastline, which accommodates all skill levels, makes it an interesting and daring place to practice watersports like surfing. The country's waves, seaside communities, and cultural diversity provide for an amazing watersport journey whether you're a novice or an expert surfer.

9.4 Rides in Hot Air Balloons

Rides in hot air balloons provide a unique and magnificent opportunity to see the nation's landscapes and photograph breathtaking aerial vistas. What you should know about hot air balloon trips in Morocco is as follows:

Hot air balloon flights are available in a number of sites around Morocco, including Marrakech, Agadir, and the High Atlas Mountains. From metropolitan skylines and lush valleys to desert vistas and harsh mountains, each area has its own distinctive beauty and attractions.

2. Best Time to Go Ballooning: Although you may go ballooning in Morocco year-round, the best time to go depends on where you are and the weather. The optimum period for hot air balloon trips in Marrakech and other lowland regions is from September to May, when the weather is cooler. Due to gentler temperatures at

higher elevations, the summer months may be preferable in the High Atlas Mountains.

3. Hot air balloon trips last around an hour on average, but the complete event, including pre-flight preparations and post-flight festivities, may last several hours. A skilled pilot will handle the balloon's height and orientation while you glide serenely over the countryside.

4. Aerial Views and Landscapes: Moroccan landscapes may be seen in breathtaking detail from the air on hot air balloon trips. You could fly above the Atlas Mountains, immense desert wastes, rich valleys, or ancient towns, depending on where you are. Keep your camera at the ready to record the stunning aerial views.

5. dawn Flights: Many of Morocco's hot air balloon trips take place in the early morning, giving you the chance to see a stunning dawn from above. The peacefulness of the flight mixed with the gentle early light makes for a very lovely experience.

6. Safety Considerations: Ballooning operators place a high priority on security and follow all applicable laws. The pilots are highly qualified, certified experts. It's critical to choose an operator with a solid reputation who adheres to safety regulations and keeps their equipment in excellent working order.

7. Dress Comfy: For your hot air balloon journey, dress comfortably and in layers. It is suggested to carry a light jacket or sweater since the air may be colder than the ground. During takeoff and landing, wear cozy shoes made for walking on rough terrain.

8. Photography and Equipment: Hot air balloon trips provide fantastic picture opportunities, so pack your smartphone or camera to record the breathtaking sights below. Make sure your gear is safe and convenient to reach throughout the journey.

9. Festive Customs: Many hot air balloon trips in Morocco come to an end with a customary celebration after landing. This often involves a Berber breakfast or tea ceremony where you may sample regional cuisine and get immersed in the native way of life.

A very unique perspective on the natural beauty and alluring landscapes of the nation may be had on hot air balloon trips in Morocco. During your balloon ride in Morocco, soar above the magnificent surroundings, feel the thrill of adventure, and make lifetime memories.

Chapter 10

Practical Tips and Resources

10.1 Essential Phrases in Moroccan Arabic

I have written a few helpful phrases in Morocco for travelers. Here are 10.1 essential phrases in Moroccan Arabic:

1. *"Salam" - Hello/greetings.*
2. *"Shukran" - Thank you.*
3. *"Afak" - Please.*
4. *"Kayn makan?" - Where is the bathroom?*
5. *"Bshwiya bshwiya" - Slowly, slowly.*
6. *"Labas?" - How are you?*
7. *"Mashi mushkil" - No problem.*

8. "Bghit ntsawar" - I want to take a picture.
9. "Kolshi bhalik" - Take care.
10. "Ana msawra mzyan" - I'm having a great time.

And here's a bonus phrase:

10.1 "Shwiya bzaf" - Very good.

Please be aware that Moroccan Arabic, also known as Darija, has regional variants, therefore depending on the precise place within Morocco, these expressions may be used in various dialects or somewhat changed.

10.2 Options for Accommodation

There are several alternatives available in Morocco for lodging to accommodate various tastes and price ranges. You may want to take into account the following typical lodging choices:

1. Hotels: Morocco offers a variety of lodging alternatives, from pricey hostels to opulent 5-star resorts. Hotels may be found in large cities, popular tourist attractions, and seaside regions. Morocco is home to several multinational hotel brands that provide a wide range of facilities and services.

2. Riads: Riads are historic Moroccan homes that have been transformed into upscale inns or bed and breakfasts. These delightful lodgings offer a more homey and genuine atmosphere and often include an inside courtyard or garden. Particularly well-liked riads may be found in Marrakech, Fez, and Chefchaouen.

3. Guesthouses: Also known as "maisons d'hôtes," guesthouses are more intimate lodgings frequently maintained by neighborhood families. They provide a more individualized and comfortable experience. Both urban and rural locations include guesthouses, which provide an opportunity to get to know the residents personally.

4. Hostels: There are becoming more hostels in Morocco, especially in well-known tourist destinations like Marrakech, Essaouira, and Tangier. Hostels are an inexpensive choice that provide both private rooms and communal dorms. They are a fantastic option for travelers or tourists wishing to connect with like-minded explorers.

5. Resorts: If you're looking for a posh, all-inclusive vacation, there are resorts in coastal cities like Casablanca and Agadir. These resorts often have private beaches, several dining options, swimming pools, and recreational facilities.

6. Campgrounds: Morocco's varied landscapes provide camping options, particularly in the arid areas like Merzouga and Zagora. You have the option of camping in your own tent or signing up for a camp in the desert that is planned and offers classic Bedouin tents.

7. Vacation Rentals: Thanks to the growth of websites like Airbnb, Moroccans are increasingly using vacation rentals. In numerous cities and towns, you may discover homes, villas, or even flats for rent.

It's usually a good idea to do your homework and make reservations for your lodging in advance, particularly during busy travel times. When deciding, take into account elements like location, facilities, cost, and reviews.

10.3 Communication and the Internet

Here are some important considerations to have in mind about internet and communication in Morocco:

1. Mobile Network Providers: Maroc Telecom, Orange, and Inwi are just a few of the country's many mobile network providers. To have access to mobile internet, calls, and SMS services, you

may buy a local SIM card from these carriers. Check to see whether your phone can use the local network frequencies and is unlocked.

2. Wi-Fi: Free Wi-Fi is available in many hotels, eateries, cafés, and public locations in popular tourist destinations and large cities. The internet connection's speed and quality, however, might differ. Check with your lodging or keep an eye out for Wi-Fi signs in public areas is a smart idea.

3. Internet cafes: These establishments are common in cities and charge customers to use their computers and access the internet. If you don't have your own device or want a dependable internet connection, they are a practical choice.

4. Voice over Internet Protocol (VoIP) and Messaging applications: Popular VoIP and messaging applications like WhatsApp, Skype, and Viber are extensively used in Morocco. These applications may be helpful for

exchanging messages, sharing images over the internet, and placing free or inexpensive calls.

5. Internet connectivity in isolated or Rural places: Internet connectivity in isolated or rural places may be restricted or less dependable. It is essential to confirm the availability of internet services in advance with your lodging or the local government.

6. Internet Speed and Data Restrictions: Although Morocco's internet infrastructure has advanced over time, your location and service provider may have an impact on the internet speed. Additionally, certain mobile data plans could contain fair use guidelines or data consumption caps that, if reached, might slow down your internet performance.

7. Public Payphones: Public payphones are still present in certain regions, although their use has declined as mobile phones have become more and more common. These payphones accept money or prepaid phone cards for calling.

If you want to use your mobile phone while traveling in Morocco, don't forget to ask your service provider about roaming fees and data plans. In case of network failures, it's also a good idea to have backup communication channels, such offline maps or a physical map.

Printed in Great Britain
by Amazon

24727761R00076